I AM A FIELD FULL
OF RAPESEED,
GIVE COVER TO
DEER AND SHINE
LIKE THIRTEEN OIL
PAINTINGS LAID
ONE ON TOP
OF THE OTHER

THE
SEAGULL
LIBRARY OF
GERMAN
LITERATURE

ULRIKE ALMUT SANDIG

I AM A FIELD FULL
OF RAPESEED,
GIVE COVER TO
DEER AND SHINE
LIKE THIRTEEN OIL
PAINTINGS LAID
ONE ON TOP
OF THE OTHER

TRANSLATED BY KAREN LEEDER

LONDON NEW YORK CALCUTTA

This publication was supported by a grant from
the Goethe-Institut, India.

Seagull Books, 2022

Originally published in German as *ich bin ein Feld voller Raps, ver-
stecke die Rehe und leuchte wie dreizehn Ölgemälde übereinandergelegt*
by Ulrike Almut Sandig © Schöffling & Co., Frankfurt, 2016

First published in English translation by Seagull Books, 2020
English translation © Karen Leeder, 2020

ISBN   978 1 8030 9 185 3

British Cataloguing-in-Publication Data
A catalogue record for this book is available
from the British Library

Typeset by Seagull Books, Calcutta, India
Printed and bound by WordsWorth India, New Delhi, India

CONTENTS

α

LAND OF BEGINNING

in the beginning there's no one.
in the Land of Beginning I lay
screaming. in the end, I lie silent
white writing on white ribbons
of the wreath. can you read it?
in the beginning, the end, that
same vowel and always lying
you hear my beginning. I am
a stream that flows into others
while others again flow into it.
I am made wholly of language
I am this wild vowel of origin
the unique defining feature
of my lost kind that must speak
to understand itself. we
are alone and now all together:
dona nobis pacem, us fragile
greedy alpha-creatures. I am
not alone, you are not alone
we stray, oh Lord, from one trial
to the next and stab each other
in the back: I have, you have
no, we have a way of always
losing track, so where is, oh
Big Bang the beginning of the
bad? in the Land of Beginning
lay my little brook with its
beak. in the beginning I lay

I was no one and no one is who
I will become. in between I am
a fluid tuning fork I am my own
song coming in **from the wings**
across a completely white field
of rapeseed covered with snow.

I

I AM A FIELD FULL OF RAPESEED

dear friends, please don't misunderstand

we don't know each other yet. I don't even know
myself. every morning up I get and don't have a clue:
is it me, Almut? Ulrike? just who was that child under
its mother's skirts? I am the mother, I am the daughter
I am the shadow for you to hide beneath
I am a field full of rapeseed, give cover to deer
and shine like thirteen oil paintings laid one on top
of the other. I am the landscape, I am the huntress
at home on the open plain, sitting in the raised hide
at the forest edge counting deer in the field. my friends
do you see my hair cropped short? I shall let it fly loose
in the wind. I am a text that begins to unravel
just as it reaches an end, just a bit of a soldier

his brows perhaps, his calves or that gallows humour
that he would lose the day he failed to give the order
to shoot to a miserable line of shivering soldiers
because he had seen in the even more miserable line
before him a pregnant girl. I am that girl.
I am the row of thirteen rifles, I am a military
court martial. I'm not a well-behaved child
that only unties her hair in secret and lets it fly loose
in the wind! I am a sprite, wild-eyed wind, child
of the skies, and turn about a tower with a high balcony
where a woman stands and secretly, silently, unties
her hair. but no, I'm not that woman there, and if I am

I never want to be her again. please understand, dear friends

I say everything twice,
do everything twice. I repeat

everything: every mistake
and every betrayal, always twice: TEST!

TEST! **I am a double-voiced song-bird
with a human face**

and it's hard to see I'm an odd bird at all
when I sit in the fern tree

and double-clink, double-
click and creak

and grind with my beak. I am
a travel company luring

you South, as if happiness
truly is buried below the equator

but don't be deceived! I can't
be trusted, or if I can then

only twice. though there's no
helping you, not even once

I'm a little two-legged teapot
wearing my father's

black cassock, his white collar
and I carry with me

my mother's girlhood dreams
when I leave you, it's

always twice:

once in the South, but just as a test
and once STOP! in the Northwest

my love,

> a little bird told me here too, so it must
> be true, that everything has its opposite.

only yesterday I saw a second Ulrike laughing
into the camera but she didn't look

> anything like me, I hardly recognized her at all.
> my love, you and me and all that exists

we could also be our opposites. I could have
a different name. how about **Hinemoana**?

> look: even if I don't move at all
> the globe keeps on turning

and always in circles. who the hell said
the Antarctic is always

> always right down below? it wasn't me
> it wasn't Hinemoana and it wasn't

you either. broad and broken
the Antarctic nudges its way

> towards Bautzener Straße
> and now I must close and remain

your Hinemoana.

> P.S. only the little bird can't find its
> opposite. a bird is always a bird

even here.

this tale is nowhere written down.
it cannot be soothed. this tale wanders
from mouth to mouth and is scared stiff
of its inventors. dark, dark it is behind the
tight-clamped teeth of the children; spit it out:
darker than the films piled on their Billy shelves
darker than all their war games put together
it wears a coat of human hair but inside
it is always too cold. it rages in the freezer
knocks on all the walls and doors and when
you come home at dawn you will find it
dripping wet. ah, that's the moment a flood
broke over the fairy tale, and shortly before
it drowned in its own tears, it told a tale
of the cruelty and pride of its inventors
but no one was listening; you were still out.

ballad of the abolition of night

underneath the utterly cloudless sky
of a state lagging somewhat behind
on the historical timeline of our kind
in a camp for detainees
night was abolished. a naked man
had his eyes bound
and against medical advice both hands
tied above his head
from time to time a man touched his skin
with a cordless drill
the report states that the man stood 2½ days

underneath the utterly cloudless sky
of a state lagging somewhat behind
on the historical timeline of our kind
in a camp for detainees
a man fetched another from his cell
dressed him in bra and thong
and led him like a dog through the room
a leather lead on his chains

and told him he could save himself
by performing doggy tricks

underneath the utterly cloudless sky
of a state lagging somewhat behind
on the historical timeline of our kind
in a camp for detainees
a man turned another on his head
and poured a cobalt-coloured
ocean into his anus. but however hard
he punched the man in the stomach
the detainee spat out nothing but water

underneath the utterly cloudless sky
of a state lagging somewhat behind
on the historical timeline of our kind
in a camp for detainees
a man smashed the head of another
against the concrete wall
then laid a cloth on his face and soaked
him for 5½ hours with water
until he only needed to snap his fingers
for the man to take a deep breath
and give him a tale of his own accord
from 1,001 nights and more

underneath the utterly cloudless sky
of a state lagging somewhat behind
on the historical timeline of our kind

in a camp for detainees
a man at the end of his shift laid
the other after the session
in a coffin that could be locked from outside
or folded him into a pile
of washing together with shoes and packed
him in a wooden crate

underneath the corrupt and cloudless sky
of a state lagging somewhat behind
on the historical timeline of our kind
in a camp for detainees
in a wooden crate there lay a man with
only one eye. with the other
he observed the completely uniform
sky that was green, so green,
and with the last shred of his human sense
he jerked, he laughed, he screamed
in a spasm he thought would never end

this is a **lullaby for all those** who resist
when it's time to go to sleep. a lullaby for all
those who put up a fight, when somebody
says: lights out, no more talking, my tired
friends, in the bars all the chairs have been
stacked on the tables, the billboards hum
as the posters change, cameras film
the empty bank foyers, all the night
kiosks are alight, all the night buses
purr through the illuminated cathedral

of the city. we're just talking in pictures. but

do we have any idea how DARKNESS
is written? my tired, my night-blind friends,
we're waiting for good news, though good
news is rare by day, we're waiting for two
or three of those good, humming dreams
four peace treaties, five apples in deep sleep
we are waiting for six cathedrals and for
those seven fat cows, eight quiet hours
full of sleep, we're waiting for nine friends
gone missing. we're counting our fingers.

we're still resisting. we won't go to sleep.

hello, did someone just say **something serious for a change?**
good night, my soul, I was already on my way, anyway
but hold on, why can I still hear you night after night
and tired, so tired, stone-tired, star-tired, hear you turning

in your grave? dear me. I'm sick to death of this spinning lark
you're a news satellite, you turn and turn about a mighty globe
in the dark, but one that doesn't quite run true
hello soul, if you were still here with me, I'd be done with you

no sign of it in Melbourne
it just kept raining all the time

in Gisborne they said they'd heard
of the South and what is more

at home on the fragile
flat roofs of June and July.

just once the South
was caught in attendance

but when it saw us, it span round
13½ times on the spot

and confided in us the secret
of its hundredth name

mark it well, it said, and in
the same moment somewhere

in the thrumming bright prospects
of our unconscious it was

gone

very slowly beneath his feet
a tectonic plate nudges its way North
above him a cliff face has been
wrinkling over millions of years
towards the shimmering clouds that
fly past at crazy speeds above ground
and cliffs and that hunter, who stands
surrounded by a flock of sheep. the mike
shakes on his arm and registers

the polyphonic songs of sheep

the sound of grass in their mouths
the snorting from their variously
coloured nostrils and how their heavy
coats brush against one another.
in the tailwind the fake fur of the mike
stirs and draws out the deeper frequencies
and this audio-hunter, arm raised
high above the swaying heads
of the sheep on the tectonic

plate that moves on without a sound.

Birdwood Avenue, Darwin 0800
I photographed a pair of black swans

drifting on the lake in the Botanical Garden
the lens of the water thick with weed

their blackness was so intense
they nearly sucked the cyan from the sky

just before I clicked the shutter
the surface seemed to shake

Birdwood Avenue, Darwin 0800
I photographed two key creatures in mourning

I mail you. you write back to say
that I have never been to Darwin

to trill a song of consolation with real animals, alone and in company, and to look that old devil fear deep in his wide-open eyes

rock-a-bye little bird
everything is good

rock-a-bye little mouse
kiss away the blood

rock-a-bye lion's mouth
all his teeth are gone

rock-a-bye dear old horse
he doesn't have a mane

and rock-a-bye-bye little hen
nothing will be good again

but then
—

my friend, she's already missing
the balcony at the top of her house

my friend, she already longs
for the cupola of papier-mâché air

where, not so long ago, swallows
circled in the exact shape of the skull

of my friend, and all for what?
all of that to sleep long, longer

and lightly, to fall as rain in a slow dive
through the earth's atmosphere

to sleep again like pain, to race towards
the naked head **of my friend**

each one of us in a bed made of nothing
but air getting hotter and hotter

above us arches the plexiglass night
we throw back our heads

and are patently standing too close
to the crossroads, where on the hour

they set off the fireworks
the first rocket shoots over

the stone figure on the fountain
and soars up into the dark sky

sprinkling it with light, the shadows
of the tallest buildings draw

in, someone applauds and we
are patently standing too close

to each other. you don't know me
yet, *mon amie*, in seven weeks

I will leave you, but not tonight.
for now it's enough that it is raining

ashes and bright, bright coloured light
onto your face, *mon amie*

not to be old and not to be young, but old
enough to be several things at once: Ulrike

and Almut, a great beast that walks upright
to be a strange beast, that can talk. amazed

at the beast that can say 'I', that can
remember. to be hungry like a beast, an

insatiable hunger for simple things like 'tree'
like 'father' and 'mother', like 'you' and 'me'

not to understand all kinds of things, but
to be old enough no longer to feel

ashamed. to be afraid of illnesses and
parents getting smaller, their laughter

in the long grass behind the house like children.
to become lighter and lighter and blow

with the wind in any direction. to put down
roots in any town. to be a tree behind

mother and father's house. to have
no name, no longer to say: 'I am'

to be wood in a table, where someone sits

II

GIVE COVER TO DEER AND SHINE

it had all been arranged. all the guests had
appeared: astrophysicists and astronauts

of renown, the Education Minister, and last
but not least: **the tattooed friends of the stars**

everyone had come. they wore glasses
of card and looked up at the sky, the sky

itself had made room for the passage of Venus
before the broad countenance of the sun

it had all been arranged. the tattooed friends of the stars
were the first to notice that something wasn't

right. after a while it dawned on the experts
too: where was Venus? where was the planetary

beauty spot on the face of our sun? no one
saw a thing. was it the date? was it the

light? the telescopes showed their images
of the transit of Venus—with the naked eye

there was nothing to be seen. the experts furrowed
their brows, the Education Minister doubted

the very idea. only the tattooed friends of the stars
laughed themselves stupid and slowly carved

dark, round figures into each other's faces

the land of plenty

good morning, Germany, turn your hazard lights on
and take it down a gear, a transporter on the A14 is

in a spin because the driver looks up too late from his
smartphone, where his girlfriend is finishing with him in
     real time

God, my heart's packed in, the driver says to himself, and
in the half-light of the hold, the freight, poultry, breaks a leg

not to mention a wing, a neck, because the transporter, at
     the mercy
of that unfortunate event, ploughs into the noise protection

barrier and anything with breath in its body is up and away,
     as if it had
always been in training just for this, it flies invisibly and in
     plain sight

and, on the count of three, those already safe in the trees jump
     out of their skin

and into a blue freedom as yet unknown: living creatures,
  horizon, basta!

instructions for flying

I   spread your arms out at shoulder height and act like you can fly.

II   be like the priest in his black cassock who, unbeknown to him, lifted up off the floor in the middle of the final blessing, flew to the belfry, fell into deep sleep, and deeper.

III   keep to the stunted hedges at the edge of the village, the banks of fog, the woods.

IV   rattle the implacable tree of history, whatever the blowback.

V   don't let yourself be hurried. and if they hurry you, take flight.

VI   don't let yourself be harried. and if they harry you, find a way out.

VII   find hiding places. climb up trees, don't build yourself a house.

VIII   be like the fly with a noose round its chitinous neck, who flew circuits in the kitchen light, until a bored kid had enough of the game. clean your wounds.

IX   climb on top of a boundary wall and jump for joy. crawl
     under the wire-mesh fences and find a way through.

X   trust in centrifugal force to get away.

XI   be like the bat that flew straight out of the window of
     the lab, without bumping into anything, after someone
     pricked out both its eyes, as part of their research into
     echolocation.

XII employ no cunning. take no comfort. count up to
     thirteen and jump.

let's forget
your splatter-nightmares.

this is reality calling. now forget the real
most of all forget the data sets from the news satellites
the moon, forget

the news itself, forget
something is tumbling towards us midway to the satellite
their feathered feet are beds being shaken
crystallographically at your tiny power of reason? forget

the pictures. it is all real and tumbling towards the pair of us.
hey, turn little circle. become crystalline, become quiet
in the coveredness of things-in-themselves.

the far side of the moon, forget
forget Fitcher's bird. no fairy tales now.

forget the forgetting, at least for the moment and
midway to the moon, forget
at least for the duration of a poem

yourself and push back your pointed hat
are the gods dangling
is someone shaking
the stories, forget

and now join in and tumble too
be a white shadow cast
be white, like white is white. know nothing.

this here is a **snowman.**
even this snow I've made for you. roll your

winter information, but forget all that informati
roll your snowball now and lose your head over it
be a tumbling in winter, a gentle falling

that you are full of foliage and quite without dosh.
you are the first and last snowman
full of joy

only much longer-lasting than

let's build one too! this snowball and
snow over the pristine surface of

on
be three times a ball!
it's not too bad, snowman

nothing is bad, nothing too grim
in your life, that will be
you tumble down through the quiet sky as

snow.

snow falls and disappears as it touches the ground
you breathe almost soundlessly. we are lying on the floor
of a northern sea under the weight of total darkness.
little sister, are you asleep? can you hear the pink noise
the roar of the ocean liners? the whales lose their way and drift
towards the brightly lit shores. from here no constellations

in sight. nor from the bottom of the ocean and not
with your eyes closed, not at night, not when it snows, and
never
in the orange glow of sky above the place you and I call
home. you breathe soundlessly. snow falls in chunks, in flakes
no, it falls apart. we are silent and drift side by side into
the trembling bottomless roar of this snow-globe world.

rooted to the spot I stood among the trees
in **the snow-globe wood** where one man was
thrashing another. I was still small, I still
did not know the tale of the Russian
that Grandfather shot so as not to be shot
by the Russian. rooted to the spot
I stood among the trees looking at one man
thrashing another as he lay there
on his back. rooted to the spot I stood
in the snow-globe wood hoping for blood
and an unmistakable cry—so that years later
I could write, I was there when it happened
and ran as fast as I could to fetch help

don't say it with roses, don't say it with flowers
at all. snowball bush, camomile or

the frost flowers in my parents' heath cottage
they are all real. but we, you and me

are we not reality-proof? say it
in fractals, say it in all the stelliformity

of the Koch snowflakes on your coat
in winter, say it on an empty sheet

of paper folded into dragon curves. say it
for me in the sound of Peano curves, say it

for me in a piece for four hands, but don't
make a meal of it, man, instead be so kind

as to look away and ignore me those days
I can't stand myself again. best would be

you don't say it to me at all. let it melt
on your tongue, slowly, this snowball

push it back and forth, I want to read it
from your lips like Mandelbrot, almond bread, fresh and
warm.

δ

LIKE

we will be at least two when it
begins. the process has started. we're
standing on the brink of the breakthrough
the dawning of a grand midday, that knows
no night. this is where we do away
with our bad-tempered mistrust, raise ourselves
to become a force to be reckoned with, raise
ourselves, erase ourselves. from now on
nothing will stand in our way, no language
we cannot master, we will strike out mistakes
and shake each other's freshly washed hands
we will be strands of DNA, we will twist
ourselves into one another, suspend
the axis of our disbelief. we're moving
towards a new system of tonal notation
that will still need decoding, we will
march together as one, bright as day
a single self-contained physical body
in its uniform but well-nigh
uncontrollable movement towards
the right. there will be an imbalance
like on the first day. well prepared we
wait for the breakthrough. we are boiling with joy

III

THIRTEEN OIL PAINTINGS

she lay in the basket and drifted along the Elbe
bobbing past Mělník and Zeithain. ultrasound waves

conveyed a completely false impression
of language: this little old man black and white

with the heart of a bird. do you remember
the way she yelled air into her lungs and how

I screamed, too, that I was a gently dug-out grave?
by midnight she was hoarse

drifted past the roots of verbs
looking up at their bent branches

and into the never-divided heaven
that kept turning quietly in space, turning, turn–

we were woken by the ear-splitting laughter

of the grey and white birds. a yellow-beaked
chattering, a squalling and cackling

as if language had once been theirs

ladies and gentlemen, if you please, listen
just to the side and beyond. follow

the sound trace of the electronic poem on its path
past the speaker boxes. can you already see

music and sound? can you already hear
the coloured lights? **the electronic poem**

is a poem within a poem and well
hidden in the wave forms of the future

that one moment later is already
our history. it hovers by the ears of Edgard

Varèse's grandchildren—and past.

this poem is perfectly transparent
it is not legible. it is as good

as not there. it hasn't been written
yet. **the perfect poem** can only be

sung and spoken, played and
heard and then played over again:

sounds in a darkened building
like inside the belly of a massive fish

made of lighted diodes. you still see nothing?
then, if you please, look just to the side—and past.

a little group   of researchers from
Hearken and Aachen   stubbornly claim that once
there was something that looked like a great and
impossibly beautiful, a singing, house with two different-
sized horns instead of a roof and, spanning from gable to
gable, its many wafer-thin walls, like otherwise only
circus tents have. oh absolute amateurs! those researchers
from Hearken and Aachen are laughed out of court. but
we believe them and scour their papers for what is known
of this house, which is this: that when you stroked it, the
doors would softly creak. that when you went in, its three-
hundred and fifty windows would begin to hum. and that
when you wandered inside, moving pictures would light
up the dark of the walls, so you could scarcely believe
your own eyes. that's what it said in all the reports. post
scriptum it should be noted that the researchers from
Hearken and Aachen called it a house. on this point, they
were sadly mistaken. in truth it was the **poem of a house.**

when the performance is over, the applause has died
down, when the very last image of the woman with
the child in her arms can no longer be seen in
the darkened hall, when the audience has returned home
and has had its own children, has brought them
up and has grown imperceptibly small, smaller, and at
last disappears, when even the hall has not stood there
for years and there exist only the blueprints and
a handful of yellowing pictures to prove how uniquely
beautiful it all was, and that inside it looked like the
belly of a massive fish and that's how it sounded too
—then after all that has gone, there's still this old
rumour, that once there was something that looked
like a great and impossibly beautiful, a singing, house
with two different-sized horns instead of a roof
and hundreds of wafer-thin   walls spanning from gable
to gable, like   otherwise only circus
tents   —

why don't we just whip it out

says the doctor **apropos the uterus**
of my mother. to my mother he says
we have to operate anyway
and while we're at it, we might as well
don't you think? why not, say the mothers
of my friends cheerfully, they reckon
they are happy, empty, ergo healthy.

but mother mine! what about the last
of that dark red light, the traces
of quiet, what's to be done with
the vestige of hair of the twin I
dreamed, but who never existed
her fingerprint the size of your tiniest vein?
mother says nothing. we look at each other

the way one only looks at one's own body

each day forgetting what we are made of:

liver and stomach and brain. apes are
what we are, who forget every day
to be **apes** and sleep each night
like creatures without their pelt.
waking with the first sound, waiting
and waking, waking and waiting
watching the windows, the visible glass

the facades of the houses. we have got
used to the emptiness inside our bodies.
we have lost track of its pet names
'inner child' or 'cardiac arrhythmia'
'demon' or 'soul'. not believing
a word of it. growing weary of it, feeling
insecure as we sleep, being awake every

night. suddenly being afraid of the dark

beatbox

click. go on, take a guess, while you are stuck here
under duress gobbling down another ditty, what's at
your back door sitting pretty, snapping a mouse's
neck or two? really got no clue? have you no scrap
of wit or have you never had a kit? of course you're
in the dark: viz. his latest lark in this catastrophic
verse, hang on there: things can only get worse. your cat
did not just chew up a mouse, right now your cat
is in the house, about to pinch those boots of yours,
without a flicker of remorse, as after all you're on
the lyric route and won't be needing any boots.
no shit: your precious kit is full of it. so now you'll see
what kind of crazy compound your precious pet has
left behind, your puss in boots, oh! and now here
comes the bit where you join in, all together now:
are you mad, you big fat cat, with those boots n' cats
n' boots n' cats n' boots n' cats n' boots n' cats n' ∏

night song

when this buzzing creature doing its rounds in the
torture chamber of a single night of the author who
could not get to sleep, this mosquito poem suddenly
looks like a sticker in the poetry album of said author
who rubs her ears next morning and cannot even
remember that this most insignificant, that is
unsophisticated, titch-of-a-midge poem ever existed,
and if only an utterly benighted group, that is a troop,
of German scholars, not unlike terminators in the
brain of said author, obstinately insist that there was
something, just now, some sort of ghost that had the
air of a giant armoured beast, now an ex-armoured
beast, a rotten thing, a monster no less, sitting on a
book that is sprayed with blood, no puff, no it is
sprayed with bluff and, look, yes, stuffed with poetry,
then this little poem too is finally toast, has become ∞

for days the air has been shifting: the trees
fling visible pollen into the eyes of Cold
Saint Sophie and into the empty sky within.
they aim for all that is invisible. the after-
noon moon, the satellites in orbit and in
their research capsules beyond Venus all
the monkeys and dogs missing without
trace. in my courtyard the horse chestnut
makes quiet gestures no one understands.
when the earth turns and North finds itself
underneath, it rains **creatures with skins and
leaves with fingers** into the universe. that's
what they say when they don't have a clue,
and that includes you. the chestnut in
my yard has been feeling its way in the dark
for days as if it is looking for grounds to
brace itself against the fall into heaven.

getting tight in this cage, don't you find? dark in the morning, a duller light. for a while now it's been dark in the morning and dark in the evening, at midday I can't see your hand in front of my face. you are made up only of absence. time and again I ask the black holes in your belly: haven't the two of us, you and me both, lost each other a long time ago. the lost girl in the Superwoman costume, the lost boy with the beer belly and bald spot. brother mine, we are still stuffed from the evening. pah, claustrophobia and pain, men don't feel such things, you say. more steak perhaps? this crumbs-on-the-path lark is getting old. dear Hansel, I am your **Gretel in a Superwoman costume** and you are really the only reason I can find to keep looking back over this shoulder of mine and at the same time keep treading the path that leads home.

almost thirteen questions about Idomeni, 2016 AD

and what if love is not the answer after all?
and what if that dove doesn't go out and
fetch the first leaf it finds and bring it
back as a sign: land in sight? and what if
there's no daylight on the waters ahead
but instead just women and children
sinking? and what if there's not a single
jot of good *Deutsch* to be found in this
Land of mine, but tarred and feathered
pity as a hyperlink, until I go and forget
my own language too? and what are you
up to? I'm drowning. and I don't mean
that ironically either. my conscience and
me, we are rarely at one. we find rhymes
for our moral dismay and do sweet FA.
what is the right question anyway? and
what if Idomeni is the only answer and a
new way of sinking between stools? do
you trust me or not, the Chancellor
retorted, falling between tables and waited

for question number nine: what makes for
a plausible case so that a man, woman and
child are not sent back home? I don't
know right from wrong. I talk about
flailing in icy water as a new form of sport.
what was the question again? and what if
dove weren't a brand you use to wash
your hands and forget in all innocence?
coocoo, coocoo, Idomeni, there's blood in
the shoe. I wash my hands in the rain.

news from the German language, 2026 AD

Berlin. if it works, I'll be a field full of
rapeseed, give cover to deer and shine like
thirteen oil paintings laid one on top of the
other. if it works right now, I'll be foam on the
syrup of iraqi dates, cubes of turkish honey,
syrian poetry, a geometric form worn smooth
and round like a pebble, meadow flowers,
bonbon-mouth, spit it out: I am the pidgin of
the clumsy lads with the glossy, black locks,
that deal out their rhymes in delicate bombs,
what'ya gawping at: no one here will go to the
dogs, but the doves. (if it doesn't work, let me
forget my language. *je suis* a field full of
monoculture, give bother to steer and turn my
back. *je suis* no longer my own *Heimatland*).
but if it works, we, that's all of you and me,
will sing a lullaby, rhyme in unison as if a
single mouth full of rapeseed, we'll be liquid
glue on white paper. we'll be light and heavy.
but more than that, we will be.

IV

LAID ONE TOP OF THE OTHER

Grimm

we wrote each other messages on raw eggs
we viewed the scratches and loops we made
on the shell as hopeful signs that, despite
what had been lost, we could write literally
anything to each other, at least on raw eggs
and in the tall buildings that swayed as if
made for shifting softly along with the bright
velocity of the earth. we wrote on raw eggs
and according to the degree of urgency
we pressed extra hard, 'til another cracked.
pah, no problemo! we had a well-nigh
limitless supply of raw eggs in the fridge.
there they sat, perfect and fragile, hanging
like balloons full of future on the horizon
beyond which the night winds blow
for ever, or so we'd heard. in our skyscrapers
it was always New Year and Easter rolled
into one, and if something came apart
the whole facade was gone in a flash
and we could see one another, hair

streaming and completely unfazed in
the crumbling ruins that collapsed round
our ears, one by one, as we had fun
smashing eggs. we raised our sticky arms
in salute and waved in greeting, then
lowered our heads to a well-nigh limitless
supply of fragments and rage most grim.

tale of the land of milk and honey

good evening, Deutschland, turn the fog lights on
we're after telling it like it is, being on cue:

those who want in must chomp their way through
a cake that's not found anywhere in Grimm;

those who want out are gone in two shakes, quicker
than the time it takes to think of a four-syllable word.

just say three times: milkandhoney, milkandhoney.
we've lost our way in your shopping malls

can't tell them apart any more. in Höxter
a fat girl buys an angel of clay and asks

at the till: what does hope mean? in Steinheim
Hakan drinks his coffee strong, he dreamed again

he swam across a honey-cake-Mediterranean
sea only to be beached at last on the streets

the brown-silt sands of the Land of Milk and Honey.
in Jena after a three-year trial a priest receives

a hefty fine, for driving into a police car
to avoid colliding with the line of demonstrators.

my homeland is not only the cities and villages . . .
it's also the doorman before them. I dreamed

he looks like Kaya Yanar and asks for the code word:
tell me the land where the donkeys have silver noses.

say it three times over: you're not getting in,
you're not getting in, you're—

Gold Marie's dream

at night I lie awake, my mother does the same.

impossibly tired, she strokes my snow-white hair

and calls breathlessly: cock-a-doo

dle-doo, the golden girl is back with

you!

whereas Mother Holle dreamed

he looked like a war veteran with a
seventy-year-old bullet in the brain: Father Kraut

she dreamed he wore a pointed hat and wanted
to cleanse his country before he went to sleep

Gold Marie's dream

at the break of day, I lie awake and listen
to the aftermath of the night's noisy dreams

a high-speed chase through our house
that was sold to strangers long ago.

at the break of day, I listen to mother. she says
what I lack in the head I make up for in the legs.
mother was as swift as an express train, nifty as

a mobile network, invisible as data transfer
oh, she was always everywhere, finger in every pie.

in the cellar the lamp goes off and back on
in the kitchen all four gas rings are alight
in the bedroom there are heaps of featherbeds.

on the nightstand, a tea-glass of ice is
not what it seems, with a jpeg embedded

and a picture of a child hidden inside that
screams: hey, mother, where have you been?

Pitch Marie's fever dream

cock-a-doodle-doo, the dirty girl
is back here too! I'm a dog, a lazy slut

but do I really give a fuck? when the bread
called take me out, take me out, or

I'll burn, I was busy contemplating
the shock front of particles in the blood-

orange solar storm, when the
apple tree called: shake me

shake me, all of us apples are
ripe, I ate one. it was sweet

like All Souls', juicy like fresh
snow. the others I left there

for the grateful starlings. I lay
in the loathsome woman's sheets

scribbling notes and thought to myself: boy
will there be trouble.

Rose Red,

father was an officer. he installed an
orgone-radiator next to our beds

that was shortly before, with me stood watch
you drowned him. if someone asks, we say

our dear father never came back from the war.
everyone nods and clocks what war we mean.

it haunts all families. makes the other wars
look bow-legged. lurks hidden in the TV-set.

me: this film was just awesome.
you: it was so shit I left half-way through.

me: the brown bear is an endangered species.
you: come on, let's take a ride on it.

me: we will never leave each other
you: never, so long as we live!

Snow White,

mother is a hysterical figure who cries at every family gathering.
her laughter rings clear as a bell through the chapel
where you are laid to rest and are, at last, as pale as folklore
has it. mother is beside herself, I tell you, and is that
not also a way to behave between the wars of our fathers?
what one has, the other will have too, she says
but what to do, from a purely medical point of view, to
get an average of your + my body temperature? we can't
even swim together, Snow White, never mind
converse. the red and white blood corpuscles are
running low—let's feed each other up! I'll feed you
from my mouth, you feed me with your spoon of snow.
we will be rosy and in mourning. the skin of our dear old bear
we will share. each of us will miss him just as much as the other.

Rose Red,

my skin is white on account of a sun allergy
and because I spend my days with the curtains drawn
and dream of planting a little square of garden.

your narrow mouth is red from the flesh of the girls
who passed us by on the toxic banks of the flooded
quarry ponds, where we spent our summers.

a brown bear was friend to us both. we each
smeared honey round his mouth in our own way.
you with your mouth, me with a spoon of snow.

where are you? I look for you at all the public baths
but never find you. though, of course, you and your
she-bear companion don't visit public baths.

you lie on the hidden banks of a brand-new lake
and beat each other gently with hazel switches, until
one of you laughs and calls out: hey, that hurt.

should you seek me, Rose Red, you will find me
on the ice-bear's back. we are standing on artificial
cliffs with an eye on the animal keeper's peephole.

we are smeared all over with honey.

Snow White,

I should be delighted to enlighten you, Snow White
on the differences between your appearance

and my own. appearance as a phase, looked
at in physical term for once: you are a pock-marked

waxing moon, a glass half full. I'm half-empty.
I stand in the shadow of our dear hysterical earth

and can't stand the sight of honey any more. I should have

liked to pass on father's final words, that was shortly
before, with you stood watch, I drowned him.

I should have liked to quiz you about the fluorescent algae
that swallowed his huge flat body

until he shone like an outdoor cinema screen
onto which I projected the only wish

I'd ever had about you:

Fitcher's Bird

I dipped myself in
a barrel of honey
slit open the bed and
rolled in the feathers.
now I am an odd
bird, nobody
knows me, I
scarcely know
myself. a globe is
stuck in my throat
I can't get it down:
a monstrous great
round chamber
of wonders racing
through the dark.
the beautiful bodies
of my sisters are
piled inside. legs still
bent where they went
to flee, breasts hacked

off and limbs and
faces eaten away.
tomorrow if I wish
(and I hope I shall)
I will get up and make
all those anew, all those
who were butchered.
go on, laugh if you like
I have dipped myself in
a barrel of honey
slit open the bed and
rolled in the feathers

the wolf and the seven kids

once there was an old she-wolf

she had seven wolf-cubs.
they tracked her through
the *Urwald* of Europe
across their sixteen yellow
pupils flickered the shifting
canopies of oak and rocket
flares from the naked
lunatics who'd lost their wits.
the blazing cities made
night vision tricky
at first and at the end
stowaways on their most
silent pads, raving
landscape, corpses in the leaves.

once there were seven cubs.
they grew up to be packs
tracked their way though
fields and forests, paws

in the prints of their
fellows, running ahead.
the naked lunatics
bared their teeth, said
there was a wolf on the
prowl, angry and alone.
once there were seven wolves.
not a single folk tale
between them, nor would
they ever have understood

auscultatory findings of an obdurate heart

my, oh my, how it beats and beats

it stutters and starts, jolts and balks
this obdurate heart will simply not

be still! it has slipped inside the clock case

my seventh and last kid, little whimpering thing
the worst possible place to hide: my own body.

my heart is a shrine. inside

a fragment, a spool, a gemstone
a spring, a bomb, a blue smurf.

hand on heart, you hear it ticking, right?

that faint tick-tock, really not? then take
this tightly rolled piece of paper.

Hans in luck,

I'm writing just t let you know I hv
all I need. this i my hand, this i my

arm, this i my eye, look closely now; it's all
still here, since you've been gone, + esp

at least 1x each of these: forehead, brain
and my bad luck. these days I keep it brief and write

to you in t voice of t white dove at t window
its mechanical 'tothineownselfbetrue' ru ru

ru, that most garrulous dove from Lucksville o Thames
who adds 1 last hopeful syllable onto each +

every one of her reports, 1x what a waste! anyway
I'm signing off. can scarcely understand a wd I say

w all this absence. apart from that I hv
all I need. dear Hans. but what are you up to?

+ esp: where r u?
ru ru

ru

juniper tree

strange bird! can't even stand to hear your own
song, that same old spooky melody in the shadow

of the juniper, where you hid yourself away, but
rather badly, if I may say. somewhere between owl

and nightmare, too bulky to trip the light fantastic
of the party charts of my kind. since I stumbled across you

there's juniper growing in the darkness of my body too.
tu-whit tu-whoo, coming for you, I want to build you a nest

in the hall of mirrors of my heart that is a ghost
like you. let's get lost in it and have a laugh

like old adversaries. at dusk we will sing with two
voices, it will be an old song, always in a single key:

the quarter tone under the middle mi, mi
like juniper tree, juniper tree, juniper . . .

come on, let's strike up laughter that is true and bright
in the thicket of our bodies, and all will be . . .

tu-whit tu-whoo

the girl who went forth to find out what fear is

I had almost got used to drones: their
precision flight in the unmanned expanse
of the atmosphere, formerly known as sky
their inner emptiness, and the simultaneous
imaginative excess of otherwise pleasant
engineers from Überlingen, who spend
their weekdays refining navigation
systems and trim their hedges on Saturday
but on the seventh day they rest.
I had almost got used to the outermost-shell
of my thinking about drones, their peculiar
predictability, in the way of metrological
phenomena like thunder or ball lightning.
I didn't know what drones sound like
perhaps a contrabass, or a distant song
as they converge on their human target
all eyes trained on the sky, formerly
known simply as weather arena.
I always imagined drones to be the
opposite of the trumpeting call of

cranes just before take-off, but at such
unimaginable distances that
I could only make them out
in the satellite search image, if at all.
in the end, though, the call of cranes
rising heavenwards in a series
of detonations had almost got me used to them.

little brother,

you did not drink at the first little brook
or you would be a tiger and tear me apart.

you did not drink at the second little brook
or you would be a wolf and devour me.

you did not drink at the third little brook
or you would be a fawn and give me away

to the hunters. but you drank at the fourth
little brook. you have become a huntsman.

little brother,

so now it's warrior of the year, is it?
shut it, brother mine. when it comes
to court they will play you the tape
of all our conversations. shut it, little
man in your tracksuit. you will not
even know the sound of your own
tiny voice, in the flaming peach fuzz,
when they quote you in all the
papers: sister mine, I am thirsty, if
only I knew where I might find a
brook that I might go and drink; I
almost think I heard one babbling.

Our Lady's Little Glass

Bad Driburg. glass museum. strip lights, dusk, three
minutes to closing. enter museum attendant.
curved nails, stubbly chin, murmurs to herself.

'I am tired and thirsty. my right eye is made of grass.
don't be afraid. I will hold it gently between two lunula
I'm already shutting down my laptop, already thinking

about the eyes of wild creatures out there on the carriageway,
shining in the glare of oncoming traffic. in their eyes are we more
than the land rushing past, grim-faced beasts without soul or skin?

I am tired and thirsty. give me a glass of gin and I
will lay my Microsoft-blue cloak about your shoulders
and locate some sorrow in the immediate vicinity—

let's find one at least—that can be eliminated, but then face
to face, and may the blessed Mother Mary in her grace
lay her light upon the carriageway like a cloak of glass.'

the sweet porridge

the final frontier. stardate 2016 AD
we find ourselves deep in the future of fairy tale.
we are the offspring of our own imaginings
each one eyeing up the latest online version
of his nearest and dearest. each one vying for sweet
sweeter sweetest porridge. what! it's gone
over the top! we hold the feeling of hunger
to be a heightened form of appetite, don't know
the words to make the little pot stop, we drink
two litres of water per day and turn the key
in the lock. for three or four days a year we
sit in front of our empty screens, offline
take things easy, take the view
that's us done, there's nothing else to do.
and while we kip the traffickers' little boats
pitch through a simmering southern sea
in the dark of our devices. the final frontier.
while we sit on our arse, they're making straight for us.

v

NO MAN'S LAND

in No Man's Land I lie
in the raw solar light
of my research station
in a northern night
where a tent stands
made of skin and bone
for me and nobody
else. here the rain
is always seeping in,
and my feet will never
get warm since the day
my head strayed too
far from the orphanage shoes.
where I am from, a woman
goes under without
a passport and turns up
to die in a homeland
whose passport she detests.
where I am now
there's a store selling nothing
a trench that's making no bones
a municipal pool where
I practise my freestyle
stark naked, since there's no one
but me to admire my fine, filthy
limbs and no one but me
to mock my technique—
skilled as an Icelandic woman
salting her fish—
of parting the water before me

Notes

PAGE 7 | **I am the shadow for you to hide beneath**

The poem was written as a response to nineteenth-century German poet Annette von Droste-Hülshoff's famous composition 'The Tower'.

PAGE 10 | **Hinemoana**

Dedicated to Hinemoana Baker, the poet from New Zealand with whom Sandig first collaborated for an anthology of poems based on the transit of Venus in 2012.

PAGE 12 | **ballad of the abolition of night**

Draws on the 'Report of the Senate Select Committee on Intelligence Committee Study of the Central Intelligence Agency's Detention and Interrogation Program', a summary of which was published in December 2014. It details systematic torture techniques used in 'Black Sites' or American detainee camps around the world, including those in Bagram, Guantanamo Bay and Abu Ghraib.

PAGE 16 | **say something serious for a change**

Refers to the German-Icelandic writer Helga M. Novak.

PAGE 20 | **to trill a song of consolation**

This poem quotes a famous traditional German nursery rhyme 'Heile heile Kätzchen' ('Heal heal little kitten'), sung to children as a get-well song.

PAGE 21 | **of my friend**

The poem is dedicated to the sound-cosmonaut Sebastian Reuter.

PAGE 30 | **instructions for flying**

This poem alludes to the leaflets that mysteriously appeared at the refugee camp in Idomeni in 2016 with instructions detailing how to find a way across the Greek border to Macedonia, provoking mass movement of refugees. The leaflets were signed Kommando Norbert Blüm, after the German minister who had visited the camp and expressed his dismay at the inhumane conditions.

PAGES 32–5 | **let's forget the far side of the moon** and **snowman let's build one too!**

These poems draw on *The Children's and Household Tales of the Brothers Grimm*. The snow comes from Mother Holle's featherbeds in the story of the same name and 'Fitcher's bird' refers to another fairy tale in the 'Grimm' cycle later in this volume.

PAGE 37 | **the tattooed friends of the stars**

A reference to the 'Transit of Venus' project.

PAGE 41 | **we will be strands of DNA**

The content and form of this poem is modelled on statements of the German right-wing populist party, Pegida.

PAGE 46 | **the electronic poem**

This along with 'the perfect poem', 'the poem of a house' and 'rumour' are inspired by composer Edgard Varèse's 'Poème électronique': a revolutionary multimedia presentation, one of the earliest electronic verses, composed for the Philips Pavilion at the 1958 Brussels World's Fair. Le Corbusier, the renowned French architect, was commissioned to design a structure to showcase a multimedia spectacle that celebrated postwar technological progress.

PAGE 52 | **beatbox**
The German word used to practise beatboxing is 'Pizzakatze' (literally, 'pizza cat').

PAGE 54 | **creatures with skins and leaves with fingers**
Folklore across central Europe celebrates various 'ice saints' whose feasts fall in the middle of May and are often associated with the last frosts of spring. 'Cold Sophie' is one of the German saints whose feast day falls on 15 May.

PAGES 56–57 | **almost thirteen questions about Idomeni, 2016** AD
After an article by Daniel Bax, 'Die Alternative heißt Idomeni', *taz am Wochenende* (12–13 March 2016). From 2014, refugees from Syria but also from Afghanistan, Pakistan and other countries of the Middle East, began to flock to the tiny border village Idomeni in order to cross the Greek border and enter the Schengen Area, often en route to Germany and Sweden. After North Macedonia and Serbia closed their borders, the transit camp at Idomeni rapidly became a huge residential camp.

'there's blood in the shoe': The phrase comes from the original, darker version of 'Cinderella' in *The Children's and Household Tales of the Brothers Grimm*, where the tell-tale shoe is full of blood when the sisters disfigure themselves in order to try and make it fit.

Grimm

This poem marks the beginning of the cycle of poems based on *The Children's and Household Tales of the Brothers Grimm*, published in two volumes in 1812 and 1815. One does not need to know the fairy tales to appreciate these poems, but German readers might identify phrases that appear as subterranean quotations, even if they don't know where they originate from. Given that this is largely not the case in English, brief notes signal the some of the references for those who might want to explore further. The German word 'Grimm' also, however, means rage: a rage that permeates the cycle as a reaction to the darkness in the collective German consciousness.

tale of the land of milk and honey

Kaya Yanar is a popular German comedian of Turkish-Arabic origin; he is well known for his multicultural take on life in Germany.

'Unsere Heimat' ('Our Homeland') was a patriotic song in former East Germany, where it was sung by official youth organizations such as the Pioneers and the Free German Youth: 'Our Homeland is not only the cities and villages; / Our Homeland is also all the trees in the forest'.

The poem refers to one of the little-known 'Tall Tales' from *The Children's and Household Tales of the Brothers Grimm*, and to the fairy tale of the same name in Ludwig Bechstein's *German Fairy Tales* (1845), depicting a land of plenty which had to be reached by eating one's way through a pot of porridge.

Gold Marie's dream

Gold Marie and Pitch Marie are the positive and negative role models respectively in the tale 'Mutter Holle' ('Mother Holle').

They fall down a well and must busy themselves with household tasks in Mother Holle's house, including taking bread from the oven, harvesting apples and shaking out Mother Holle's 'feather-beds' (a metaphor for snow). As their names suggest, they each receive their just deserts.

PAGES 69–72 | **Rose Red** and **Snow White**

These poems appear as a dialogue between the two sisters from 'Schneeweißchen und Rosenrot', who are dissimilar in almost every way but are bound to each other; they take pity on a fearsome bear who in truth is a prince under a spell.

PAGE 73 | **Fitcher's Bird**

In 'Fitcher's Vogel' (a gruesome story, not unlike the more familiar 'Bluebeard'), the clever daughter saves herself from a bloody end brought about by her curiosity, by disguising herself as a bird in honey and feathers. She then restores her murdered sisters to life.

PAGES 75–77 | **the wolf and the seven kids** and **auscultatory findings of an obdurate heart**

Both these poems refer to the story 'Der Wolf und die sieben jungen Geißlein' in which one of the seven goat-kids memorably hides from the wolf in a clock case and survives.

PAGE 78 | **Hans in luck**

The poem draws on the fairy tale 'Hans im Glück', about the foolish boy who is always happy, despite having everything being gradually taken away from him. Many well-known writers contributed stories to the Grimms' collection, including Jenny von Laßberg (Annette von Droste-Hülshoff's sister). She was called Hans in letters from her sister. The famous quotation in the German:

'Über allen Gipfeln is Ruh' ('O'er all the hill tops is peace') comes from Goethe's iconic poem 'Wanderer's Nightsong II'.

PAGE 79 | juniper tree

Refers to the story 'Vom Machandelboom' in which a bird reveals the true nature of a mother's murderous actions in its songs. In German 'kiwitt', part of the bird's song, is also the sound made by a tawny owl and is associated with evil spirit luring one to death (or 'kiwitt, komm mit').

PAGE 80 | the girl who went forth to find out what fear is

In Grimm's 'Märchen von einem, der auszog das Fürchten zu lernen', it is a boy who sets out to test himself through various gruesome trials, in order to discover something that will make him afraid.

PAGE 82 | little brother

The poem is based on the tale 'Brüderchen und Schwesterchen' ('Little Brother and Little Sister') in which the brother is unable to resist the temptations of the forest until he is turned into a deer and killed by the King's hunt. In September 2014, Germany witnessed the first-ever trial of a 20-year-old Jihadist who had returned to Frankfurt after spending six months with IS militants in Syria.

PAGE 84 | Our Lady's Little Glass

Based on a little-known story 'Muttergottesgläschen', which tells of the appearance of the Virgin Mary to a weary wagoner. He gives her wine to drink in a flower, and she frees the wagon for him. The flower, field bindweed, is also known in English as 'Our Lady's Little Glass'.

PAGE 85 | **the sweet porridge**

'Vom süßen Brei', the story of a magic porridge pot, not unlike the broom in the story of the 'Sorcerer's Apprentice'; it also refers to the cult sci-fi classic *Star Trek*.

PAGE 89 | **where I am now**

A reference to Helga M. Novak.

Acknowledgements

Some of these poems, or earlier versions of them, have appeared in *Communion*, *Cordite*, *Poetry Review*, *New England Review*, *PN Review*, *Poetry Review*, *Shearsman*, *The German Riveter* and *The White Review*, or were read on BBC Radio 'Mother Tongue', curated by Helen Mort in July 2017. The 'Grimm' cycle of poems was published with specially commissioned artwork in a limited-edition chapbook by Hurst Street Press in 2018.

*

Thanks are due to those who supported work on this manuscript. The earliest translations go back to a commission from Poet in the City; some translations were included in submissions that were recognized by the Literarisches Colloquium Berlin, the American PEN Heim Award committee, and the judges of the English PEN EUNIC New Literary Voices Award. Subsequent commissions and invitations from Heike Bartel, Rebecca Braun, the Dylan Thomas House, Swansea and Oxford Translation Day helped the project on its way. Shoshana Kessler's enthusiasm for the 'Grimm' cycle was crucial in the final stages.